HAIKU
THE POETRY OF NATURE

EDITED BY

David Cobb

UNIVERSE PUBLISHING
NEW YORK

Frontispiece: Kitagawa Utamaro, Balloon-Flower with Other Plants, and Grasshopper, from *Picture-Book of Selected Insects*, vol. 2, 1788; colour-printed, with mica and gauffrage.

First published in the United States of America in 2002
by UNIVERSE PUBLISHING
A division of Rizzoli International Publications, Inc.
300 Park Avenue South
New York, NY 10010

2002 2003 2004 2005 2006 2007 / 10 9 8 7 6 5 4 3 2 1

Printed and bound in Hong Kong
by C & C Offset

ISBN 0-7893-0826-6

Library of Congress Control Number: 2002104714

Universe editor/jacket and endpaper design by Jessica Fuller
Designed by Peter Ward
Typeset in Centaur

CONTENTS

ACKNOWLEDGEMENTS

Sakaguchi Akiko helped to check the validity of existing translations and transliterations, and sometimes collaborated with David Cobb in creating new ones. She also provided the haiku in Japanese characters, which involved representing haiku calligraphy (*shikishi*) using a word processor, a complex creative task. Many of the translations are R.H. Blyth's and we therefore owe special thanks to the Hokuseido Press for permission to use them, and for allowing us to edit them to a more contemporary standard of layout and punctuation. We are grateful also to the other translators named below for permitting us to use their work. Laura Brockbank of The British Museum Press did sterling work searching out the right pictures among the British Museum's enormous collection.

TRANSLATION CREDITS

R.H. Blyth: pp. 10, 13 (top), 20, 24, 32 (top), 38 (top), 42 (top), 45 (bottom), 47 (top), 53, 54, 59 (bottom), 60 (top), 63 (bottom), 64 (top), 68, 72, 80 (top), 82 and back cover; Kaj Falkman: p. 13 (bottom); Lee Gurga and Emiko Miyashita: pp. 17 (bottom), 32 (bottom), 64 (bottom), 67, 75 (bottom); Kōkō Katō and David Burleigh: p. 36 (top); Ban'ya Natsuishi: p. 38 (bottom); Haruo Shirane: pp. 48 (bottom), 63 (top); Makoto Ueda: pp. 31 (bottom), 41 (bottom), 47 (bottom), 56 (bottom), 59 (top); and Ogino Yōko: p. 14 (bottom). The remainder are translated by David Cobb.

INTRODUCTION

ONE CAN *know* the main facts about Japanese haiku without having much feeling for them; and one can *feel* quite deeply about haiku without knowing many facts – intuition sometimes supplies important insights. But we imagine our reader to be someone who wants to both know something and feel something about haiku. This introduction therefore starts with an outline of the history and development of haiku in Japan, and moves on to the appreciation of haiku's aesthetic qualities.

The history and development of haiku poetry

IN JAPANESE literature we recognise certain poems as haiku as far back as the 12th century, but it was not until the end of the 19th century that the term 'haiku' was actually applied to any of these poems from the seven hundred intervening years. This is because the haiku gradually evolved almost as a by-product of other poetic activities, in particular *renga*.

Renga has complex rules, governing both form and content. Rather like an erudite 'party game', a *renga* was composed by a group who spent a period of time together, hours at least, with a leader who set the tone for the composition and decided which verses were acceptable. The final product was a chain of stanzas, with alternating lengths of seventeen and fourteen syllables.

Seventeen-syllable links normally consist of three phrases: a five-syllable phrase followed by one of seven syllables, and then five again. Fourteen-syllable links break down into only two phrases each of seven syllables. The fascination of five-syllable and seven-syllable phrases for the

Japanese goes back to the Heian period (AD 794–1185) and is innate to the Japanese language. R.H. Blyth (1898–1964), the British haiku scholar, speculated that their original appeal was 'partly because the repetition of five and the repetition of seven expressed the regularity of nature, and the alternation of five and seven its irregularity'.

As to content, *renga* poets follow strict rules, specifying topics that must or must not appear at various points in the chain. For example, Bashō stipulated that the moon should be mentioned three times in thirty-six links. But beyond the formal structure, *renga* relies for its effect on 'fragrance': each succeeding link should yield some aftermath of the one preceding it, but shift the context, and the completed *renga* should have a beginning, a middle, and a finale.

The first link, known as the *hokku*, was of crucial importance, setting the tone and style of language, the mood, and the seasonal context of the whole. It was often of higher quality, perhaps because planned carefully in advance, than the more spontaneous stanzas that followed it. It might be detached from the rest of the *renga* and put into an anthology, and so it acquired an independent existence. It was but a step from this to the increasingly common practice of creating *hokku* which were intended from the outset to be free-standing.

Individual poets contributed to the transition from *renga* to haiku. Sōgi (1421–1502) insisted that *renga* should be imbued with lofty thought (*yūgen*). Sōkan (d. 1539/40) developed a more 'popular' style of *renga*, known as *haikai no renga*, which was less formal and more accessible to ordinary people. He also emphasised sincerity. In the late 17th century several poets, above all Bashō and Onitsura, redeemed the *haikai no renga* which had become increasingly mundane and tasteless. Bashō's poetics, emphasising such virtues as directness, truthfulness and a light touch, and finding spiritual moments in the everyday lives of common people and their engagement with nature, have influenced generations of haiku writers ever since.

Although other great masters arose – notably Buson (1716–84) and Issa (1762–1826), making their reputations on the basis of individual *hokku*, not as *renga* masters – both forms had once more degenerated by the second half of the 19th century; and with the opening up of Japan to the world in the Meiji period after 1868, the influence of Western poetry threatened the future of these traditional Japanese poetic forms.

Onto this literary scene came the reformist critic and poet, Masaoka Shiki (1867–1902), who awarded literary status only to the independent *hokku* and began to use the term 'haiku' to describe the self-sufficient seventeen-syllable poem. Shiki believed that the objective style of sketching practised by certain Western artists offered hope for the regeneration of haiku, inventing for this the term *shasei* ('verbal sketching'). He insisted that haiku about actual things and events in our daily lives were generally superior to anything the imagination could invent. Upon Shiki's death, haiku poets in Japan became divided between those who thought his work of reform was complete, and those who saw it as an ongoing process: groups calling themselves 'traditionalists', 'modernists' and 'avant-gardistes' have formed, all represented in this anthology alongside the 'classical' writers.

Further information about the development of Japanese haiku may be gleaned from the Biographical Notes on pp. 85–8.

The formal characteristics of Japanese haiku

WHEN THE strictest rules are observed, there are three requirements of a Japanese haiku:

BREVITY AND COMPRESSION: a haiku should consist only of essential words, making a total of *approximately* seventeen syllables. (The Japanese idea of a syllable is quite different from that of someone speaking a European language; for example, the letter n may count as a separate syllable, whilst a syllable containing a long vowel, indicated by a macron, e.g. ō, counts as two.) Sometimes a number of syllables smaller or larger than seventeen seems either 'sufficient' or 'necessary'. Here are some examples of counts:

ō ō to (5) *iedo tataku ya* (7) *yuki no mon* (5) (= 17 in total) (Kyorai)
ichinichi mono iwazu nami oto (= 13) (Santōka)

SEASONAL FEELING: it should be possible to place the haiku in one of the five seasons of the year (five, because in Japan the New Year is reckoned to be a season in its own right). One key word, known as a *kigo*, acts as a general evocation of nature or human activities at this time of year. Poets who wish to observe this tradition carry about with them an almanac known as a *saijiki*, which they use to find season words appropriate to the time of composition. For example, on its own the word 'moon' (*tsuki* in Japanese) evokes an autumnal scene – the full harvest moon. The Japanese reader therefore understands the following as an autumn poem:

imo wo niru   *nabe no naka made*   *tsukiyo kana*   (Kyoriku)
even to the saucepan where potatoes are boiling a moonlit night

If another time of year is intended, the poet will need to specify it – 'the spring moon', 'the summer moon', etc.

Nowadays, when many of us do not live close to nature, wider interests need to be represented in haiku, so some compilers of *saijiki* include a category of 'seasonless haiku' or 'human affairs'. Lyrical haiku about the moon and cherry blossom retain their popularity, but haiku has long had a place also for topics as sombre as homelessness and illness.

A 'CUTTING WORD', called a *kireji*, is also required. This may be placed at the end of any of the three lines. If it is at the end of the first or second line, it acts as a combination of lacuna and ligature, dividing the poem into two 'unequal halves' ('unequal' in that one section is of twelve syllables and the other of only five, yet 'halves' because they achieve a degree of parity). Its use indicates to the reader a need for reflection, or invests the poem with a certain mood. For example, in the following haiku by Shiki, *ya* at the end of the first line is the *kireji*. It has no 'meaning' other than to create a pregnant pause and a sense of questioning expectation about what may be about to follow.

| *harusame* **ya** | *kasa takahiku ni* | *watashibune* |
| spring rain – | umbrellas up and down | in the ferry boat |

A *kireji* at the very end indicates attitude without, of course, creating a pause. In the following, by Bashō, *kana* is the cutting word. It heightens the emotion by signalling the poet's wonder and surprise at what he has just observed.

| *kagerō no* | *waga kata ni tatsu* | *kamiko* **kana** |
| heat waves | shimmer on the shoulders | of my paper robe |

Appreciating haiku

WITH THE season word unlocking the reader's own personal store of experience, and the cutting word inviting the reader to search for unstated connections, the haiku has been styled 'the half-said thing' (Bashō again: 'Is there any good in saying everything?'). The appreciation of haiku is a matter of collaboration between poet and reader, the one (to use a metaphor from photography) exposing something to the light, and the other developing it. As well as being half-stated, it is also under-stated, with sparing resort to the eye-catching metaphor or the subjective attribute, which might be said to be typical of much Western poetry. Haiku aims to be plain and simple, but at the same time subtle.

There is a shared understanding behind virtually all haiku that the transience of life and earthly things is made acceptable because there are also cycles of events (the seasons of the year, the wheel of human life) which turn and return. There may therefore be a sort of compact between poets and their audiences, an implicit understanding that 'every day is a good day', or at least that there is always some detail in the life going on around us which is worthy of our regard, respect and possibly celebration. Awareness and acceptance are hallmarks of haiku and they result in an affirmative attitude to, for example, solitude (without melancholy), loss, and even pain. This outlook permeates the haiku in this book.

How this selection was made

THE PICTURES in this book – all from the excellent collection of Japanese art in The British Museum – originally had no direct connection with the poems printed next to them. They do however make use of a common fund of images, sometimes having other qualities which they share with haiku: elimination of the inessential, spontaneity, positive use of vacant space, an asymmetrical balance. We have attempted to represent different styles of haiku, as well as specimens which interact in an interesting way with the accompanying pictures and with each other. It was appropriate to observe the seasonal arrangement of haiku used in a Japanese anthology, but the few New Year haiku are placed at the end of winter, rather than in the orthodox first position, before spring (in Japan the New

Year used to be in February). The translations are from a variety of hands (see Acknowledgements).

Divisions in both the calligraphy and transliterated versions of haiku are arbitrary. The calligraphy aims to please the eye, the transliteration to show how the haiku might be phrased when read aloud. If both are divided into three sections, they may be taken to coincide, but it would have been unsatisfactory to make this arrangement a general rule.

Haiku as world poetry

HAIKU has now been adopted, usually with some necessary modifications, as a poetic form in many of the world's languages and literatures (see the suggestions for Further Reading and the list of Resources on pp. 89–90).

Katsushika Hokusai, Snowy Morning at Koishikawa,
from *Thirty-Six Views of Mt Fuji*, 1830–33; woodblock.

SPRING

yuki tokete   mura ippai no   kodomo kana

snow melts
and the village floods
with children

Issa

雪
と
け
て

村
一
ぱ
い
の

子
ど
も
哉

9

akebono ya   mugi no hazue no   haru no shimo

the dawn of day –
on the tip of the barley leaf
the frost of spring

Onitsura

麦
の
葉
末
の

春
の
霜

曙
や

白
鶺

yamadori no   o wo fumu haru no   irihi kana

treading on the tail
of the copper pheasant
the setting sun of spring

Buson

尾
を
ふ
む

春
の
入
日
哉

山
鳥
の

Keisai Masayoshi, Silver Pheasants, from *Picture Collection of Imported Birds*, vol. 1, 1789; woodblock with gauffrage.

kore wa kore wa to bakari   hana no yoshino yama

'Ah!' I said, 'Ah!'
it was all that I could say –
the cherry flowers of Mt Yoshino!

Teishitsu

是は是はと
ばかり
花の吉野山

hana no kage   aka no tanin wa   nakari keri

in the shadow of the cherry blossom
complete strangers
there are none . . .

Issa

花の陰
あかの他人は
なかりけり

Utagawa Hiroshige, Embankment of the Sumida River, Edo,
from *Thirty-Six Views of Fuji*, 1859 (?); woodblock.

kake izuru koma mo ashi kagu sumire kana

frisking horses
also sniff at their legs
wild violets

Chiyo-ni

駒
も
足
嗅
ぐ

す
み
れ
か
な

駈
出
る

*atsui yubune ni chibusa no nai mune wa tsumetai
shunrai ga todoroku**

hot bath water
cold on the breastless side
spring thunder

Ogino Yōko

乳
房
の
な
い
胸
は

冷
た
い

春
雷
が
轟
く

熱
い
湯
槽
に

* The Japanese is not a haiku, but a literal translation
of an English original.

Mori Shūhō, Horses (detail), late 18th century;
four-fold screen; ink and *gofun* on paper.

Utagawa Toyokuni, A Picnic on the Beach,
c. 1795–1800; woodblock (triptych print).

hirou mono   mina ugoku nari   shio higata

on the ebb tide beach
everything we pick up
is alive

Chiyo-ni

拾ふもの
みな動くなり
塩干潟

haru sabishi   nami ni todokanu   ishi wo nage

spring loneliness –
it falls short of the surf
this stone I toss

Suzuki Masajo

波にとどかぬ
石を投げ

春淋し

amagumo ni   hara no fukururu   kaeru kana

rain clouds —
the frog
puffs his belly out!

Chiyo-ni

雨雲に
はらのふくるる
蛙かな

yūzen to shite   yama wo miru   kawazu kana

serenely
gazing up at the mountain —
a toad

Issa

いうぜんとして
山を見る
蛙哉

Hoji, Frog, from *Picture-Album by Celebrated Artists*,
vol. 3, 1814; colour-printed.

ezōshi ni   shizu oku mise ya   haru no kaze

the paper-weights
on the picture books in the shop –
the spring wind!

Kitō

絵
草
紙
に

鎮
置
く
店
や

春
の
風

harukaze ni   shiri wo fukaruru   yaneya kana

the spring wind –
the skirts of the thatcher
are blown about

Issa

春
風
に

尻
を
吹
か
るゝ

家
根
屋
哉

Katsushika Hokusai, Ejiri in Suruga Province,
from *Thirty-Six Views of Mt Fuji*, 1830–33; woodblock.

uguisu ni   temoto yasumen   nagashimoto

the songbird's song —
it stops what I am doing
at the sink

Chigetsu

鶯に
手もと休めむ
ながしもと

Kanō Yukinobu (attrib.), Bird and Flowers,
late 16th to early 17th century; hanging scroll painting.

iroiro no   na mo muzukashi ya   haru no kusa

all the various
difficult names –
the weeds of spring

Shadō

いろいろの
名もむづかしや
春の草

yoku mireba   nazuna hana saku   kakine kana

looking carefully,
a shepherd's purse is blooming
under the fence

Bashō

よく見れば
薺花咲く
垣根哉

Kubo Shumman, Gathering Spring Flowers,
c. 1800; woodblock (*surimono* print).

kyō nite mo   kyō natsukashi ya   hototogisu

even in Kyoto
when I hear the cuckoo
I long for Kyoto

Bashō

京にても
京なつかしや
時鳥

haru hitori   yari nagete   yari ni   ayumi yoru

alone in the spring —
hurling a javelin, and then
walking after it

Nomura Toshirō

春ひとり
槍投げて
槍に
歩み寄る

Katsushika Hokusai, Cuckoo and Azaleas,
c. 1834; woodblock.

kuraki yori   kuraki ni iru ya   neko no koi

in from the dark
and out into the dark –
that's a cat in love!

Issa

聞より
聞に入るや
猫の恋

ōneko no   dosari to netaru   uchiwa kana

a great big cat
flopped out asleep
on a round paper fan

Issa

大猫の
どさりと寝たる
団扇かな

Katsukawa Shunshō, Cat Licking its Paw (detail),
c. 1789–92 (?); hanging scroll; ink and colour on paper.

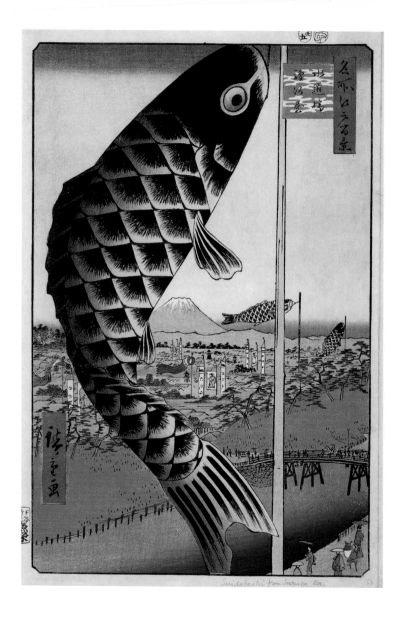

Suidobashi Surugadai

SUMMER

yūdachi ni　utaruru koi no　atama kana

summer rain –
it drums on the heads
of the carp

Shiki

　　　　夕
　　　　立
　　鯉　に
　　の
　　　う
あ　　た
た　　る
ま　　ゝ
か
な

tsuyoshi seinen　higata ni　tamanegi　kusaru hi mo

strong are the youngsters
even on a day when onions
rot on the dry beach

Kaneko Tōta

　　　　　強
　　　　干　し
　　　　潟　青
葱　　に　年
る
日
も
　玉
　葱

Utagawa Hiroshige, Suidō Bridge and Surugadai,
from *One Hundred Famous Views of Edo*, 1857; woodblock.

yūdachi ni   hitori soto miru   onna kana

a summer shower —
a woman sits alone
gazing outside

Kikaku

夕立に
ひとり外見る
女かな

hito wa nusumedo   mono wa nusumazu   sudare maku

I have stolen a man
but never a thing of value
I roll up the bamboo blind

Suzuki Masajo

人は盗めど
ものは盗まず
簾巻く

Kaburaki Kiyokata, Woman and Plantain,
late 1890s—early 1900s; album leaf (?);
ink, colour and gold on silk.

minasoko no   kusa ni kogaruru   hotaru kana

longing for the grass
at the bottom of the pool
those fireflies

Buson

水底の
草にこがるゝ
ほたる哉

shimizu suzushi   hotaru no kiete   nani mo nashi

cool clear water
and fireflies that vanish
that is all there is . . .

Chiyo-ni

清水すゞし
蛍のきえて
なにもなし

Shiokawa Bunrin, Fireflies over a River,
c. 1875 (?); hanging scroll; ink and gold on silk.

35

inazuma no naka inazuma no hashiri keri

lightning
running down inside
lightning

Inahata Teiko

wankyoku shi   kashō shi   bakushinchi no   marason

buckling in the heat
where the A-bomb burst
a marathon

Kaneko Tōta

Utagawa Kunisada (Toyokuni III), A Sudden Summer Shower,
c. 1848–52; woodblock (triptych print).

fūryū no   hajime ya   oku no taue uta

the beginning of poetry:
the song of the rice-planters
in the province of Ōshū

Bashō

風流の
はじめや
奥の田植唄

mizu ni   kage aru   tabibitodearu

on the water
the reflection
of a wanderer

Santōka

水に
影ある
旅人である

Kō Sūkei, Rice-Planting and Mt Fuji,
late 18th to early 19th century; hanging scroll;
ink and colour on silk.

nikai kara   yanebune maneku   uchiwa kana

beckoning from upstairs
to a house boat below
a round paper fan . . .

Shiki

屋根舟まねく
二階から
団扇かな

dore mo kuchi utsukushi banka no jazu ichidan

every one of the mouths
is beautiful — late in summer
a jazz group

Kaneko Tōta

どれも
口美し
晩夏の
ジャズ一団

Kitagawa Utamaro, The Male Geisha Ogie Matsuzō,
c. 1792; woodblock.

kiyo taki ya   nami ni chirikomu   aomatsuba

a clear waterfall –
into the ripples
fall green pine-needles

Bashō

清滝や
波にちりこむ
青松葉

ochikochi ni   taki no otokiku   wakaba kana

fresh young leaves –
the sound of a waterfall
both far and near

Buson

滝の音聞く
若葉かな

遠近に

友禅筆
武禅寫

Suminoe Buzen, Mt Fuji and Shiraito Falls (after Yūzen),
late 18th century; hanging scroll; ink and light colour on paper.

Hosoda Eishi, The Chinese Beauty Yang Guifei,
c. 1800–10; hanging scroll; ink, colour and gold on silk.

ōgi nite   shaku wo toraseru   botan kana

the peony
it had to be measured
with a fan

Issa

扇にて
尺をとらせる
牡丹かな

yūgao no hana de   hana kamu musume kana

the young girl
blows her nose
in the evening-glory

Issa

夕顔の
花で
洟かむ
娘かな

Utagawa Toyokuni II, Carp, *c.* 1828–34;
album leaf (?); ink, slight colour and gold on silk.

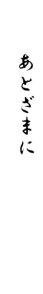

atozama ni   kouo nagaruru   shimizu kana

the little fish
carried backwards
in the clear water

Kitō

ake yasuki   yo wo iso ni yoru   kurage kana

the short night ending –
close to the water's edge
a jellyfish

Buson

natsu mushi ya   yagaku no hito no   kao wo utsu

summer insects
strike at the midnight hour
the student's face

Shōha

夏虫や
夜学の人の
顔を打つ

natsu kusa ya   tsuwamonodomo ga   yume no ato

summer grasses . . .
traces of dreams
of ancient warriors

Bashō

兵どもが
夢の跡
夏草や

Nishiyama Hōen, Procession of Insects,
19th century; hanging scroll painting.

49

hiru no ka wo   ushiro ni kakusu   hotoke kana

mosquitoes by day —
the Buddha hides them all
behind his back

Issa

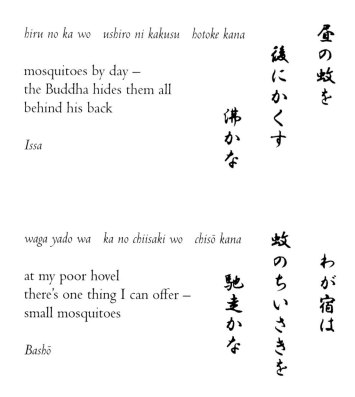

昼
の
蚊
を
後
に
か
く
す
沸
か
な

waga yado wa   ka no chiisaki wo   chisō kana

at my poor hovel
there's one thing I can offer —
small mosquitoes

Bashō

蚊
の
ち
い
さ
き
を
馳
走
か
な

わ
が
宿
は

Kaigetsudō Ando, Courtesan Entering a Mosquito Net,
c. 1705–15; hanging scroll (mounted as a panel);
ink, colour and gold on paper.

Utagawa Hiroshige, Night View of the Eight Famous Places
of Kanazawa, Musashi Province, 1857; woodblock (triptych print).

AUTUMN

meigetsu ya   ike wo megurite   yomosugara

the moon:
I wandered around the pond
all night long

Bashō

名月や
池をめぐりて
夜もすがら

imo wo niru   nabe no naka made   tsukiyo kana

even to the saucepan
where potatoes are boiling –
a moonlit night

Kyoriku

芋を煮る
鍋の中まで
月夜かな

shiratsuyu no   tama fungaku na   kirigirisu

grasshopper –
do not trample to pieces
the pearls of bright dew

Issa

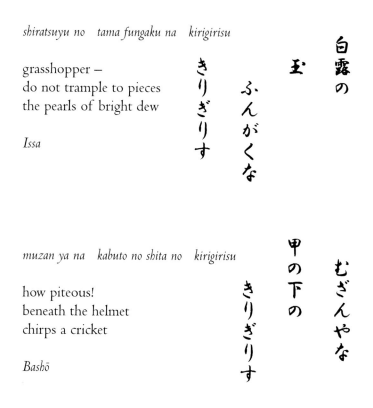

muzan ya na   kabuto no shita no   kirigirisu

how piteous!
beneath the helmet
chirps a cricket

Bashō

Kitagawa Utamaro, Balloon-Flower with Other Plants,
and Grasshopper, from *Picture-Book of Selected Insects*,
vol. 2, 1788; colour-printed, with mica and gauffrage.

shira tsuyu mo   kobosanu hagi no   uneri kana

bush-clover flowers —
they sway but do not drop
their beads of dew

Bashō

白露も
こぼさぬ
萩の
うねり哉

kare ichigo   ware ichigo   aki fukami kamo

he says a word,
and I say a word — autumn
is deepening

Kyoshi

彼一語
我一語
秋深みかも

Suzuki Harunobu, Flirtation,
c. 1768—70; woodblock.

meigetsu ya   usagi no wataru   suwa no umi

the harvest moon –
rabbits go scampering
across Lake Suwa

Buson

hosusuki ya   hosoki kokoro no   sawagashiki

plumes of pampas grass –
the helpless tremblings
of a lonely heart

Issa

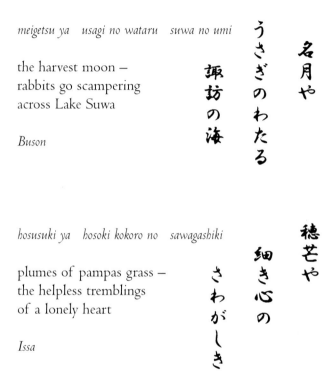

Anon. (Rimpa school), Rabbits and Autumn Grasses (detail),
18th century; six-fold screen; ink, colours and gold leaf on paper.

kishamichi ni   hikuku kari tobu   tsukiyo kana

low over the railroad
wild geese flying –
a moonlit night

Shiki

月
夜
哉

低
く
雁
飛
ぶ

汽
車
道
に

ichigyō no   kari ya hayama ni   tsuki wo insu

on the mountain crests
a line of wild geese
and the moon's seal

Buson

端
山
に

月
を
印
す

一
行
の
雁
や

Kubo Shumman, Descending Geese in Autumn,
c. 1800, woodblock with gauffrage and
applied metal dust (*surimono* print).

歌いづれ
小町をどりや
伊勢踊

uta izure   komachi-odori ya   ise-odori

which song is better –
that of the Komachi Dance?
or the Ise Dance?

Teitoku

秋たつや
何におどろく
陰陽師

aki tatsu ya   nani ni odoroku   onmyōji

the beginning of autumn:
what is the fortune-teller
looking so surprised at?

Buson

Torii Kiyonaga, A Girl Dancing with Shell Clappers under her Feet,
c. 1784; woodblock.

nusubito ni   torinokosareshi   mado no tsuki

the thief
left it behind –
the moon at the window

Ryōkan

盗人に

とりのこされし

窓の月

yagate kuru mono ni banshū no isu hitotsu

late autumn –
a single chair waiting
for someone yet to come

Arima Akito

やがて来る者に

晩秋の

椅子一つ

Utagawa Hiroshige, Seba, *c.* 1840; woodblock.

66

WINTER

dōshitemo   ochiba fumaneba   yukenu michi

no escaping it –
I must step on fallen leaves
to take this path

Suzuki Masajo

落葉踏まねば

行けぬ路

どうしても

Suzuki Harunobu, Clearing Storm at Asakusa,
c. 1766–70; woodblock.

no ni yama ni   ugoku mono nashi   yuki no asa

on moor and mountain
nothing stirs
this morn of snow

Chiyo-ni

ō ō to   iedo tataku ya   yuki no mon

'Yes! Yes!' I cried,
but someone still knocked
on the snow-mantled gate

Kyorai

Utagawa Hiroshige, Mountain River on the Kiso Road, 1857;
woodblock (triptych print).

kaze ichijin   mizutori shiroku   miyuru kana

かぜ一陣

水鳥白く

見ゆるかな

a sudden squall
and the bird by the water
is turning white

Buson

Oda Kaisen, Egret on a Willow,
19th century; hanging scroll painting.

tsuribito no   jō no kowasa yo   yūshigure

the angler —
his dreadful intensity
in the evening rain!

Buson

釣人の
情のこはさよ
夕しぐれ

umi kurete   kamo no koe   honoka ni shiroshi

the sea darkens —
the voices of the wild ducks
are faintly white

Bashō

海くれて
鴨の声
ほのかに
しろし

Katsushika Hokusai, Viewing Sunset over Ryōgoku Bridge from the Ommaya
Embankment [Edo], from *Thirty-Six Views of Mt Fuji*, 1830–33; woodblock.

akegata ya   shiro wo torimaku   kamo no koe

day breaks –
quacks of the wild ducks
surround the castle

Kyoriku

katchū no   mugon no retsu ni   fukaki fuyu

into the ranks
of the suits of armour
deep winter*

Arima Akito

* Written by the poet at the Tower of London.

Katsushika Hokusai, Ducks in Flowing Water, 1847;
hanging scroll; ink and colour on silk.

mizubana ya   hana no saki dake   kure nokoru

my runny nose —
everywhere but on its dewdrop
the twilight fades

Ryūnosuke

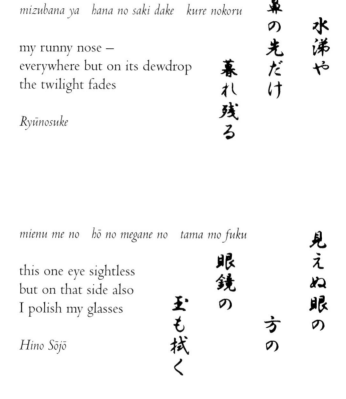

mienu me no   hō no megane no   tama mo fuku

this one eye sightless
but on that side also
I polish my glasses

Hino Sōjō

Tōshūsai Sharaku, The Actor Ichikawa Ebizō, 1794;
woodblock with powdered mica ground.

Katsushika Hokusai, Umezawa Manor in Sagami Province,
from *Thirty-Six Views of Mt Fuji*, 1830–33; woodblock.

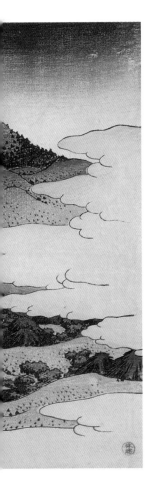

tsuru no asobi　kumoi ni kanau　hatsu hi kana

鶴のあそび

雲井にかなふ

初日哉

it's play for the cranes
flying up to the clouds
the year's first sunrise . . .

Chiyo-ni

hakidame e　tsuru ga orikeri　waka no ura

掃きだめへ

鶴が下りけり

和歌の浦

at the beauty spot
the cranes alight
on litter

Issa

79

hatsu yume ya   himete katarazu   hitori emu

the first dream of the year –
I kept it a secret
and smiled to myself

Shō-u

初夢や
秘めて語らず
一人笑む

hi no hikari   kesa ya iwashi no   kashira yori

the first gleam
of a new day
on pilchards' heads

Buson

日の光
今朝や
鰯の
かしらより

Miyagawa Chōshun, Pastimes of the New Year (detail),
c. 1724–44; handscroll; ink, colour and gold on paper.

ganjitsu ya   kinō ni tōki   asaborake

the dawn of New Year's Day –
yesterday
how far off!

Ichiku

元日や

昨日に遠き

朝ぼらけ

Eishōsai Chōki, New Year Sunrise,
c. 1795; woodblock.

BIOGRAPHICAL NOTES

In Japan the family name is put before the personal name (the latter, for poets, often a pseudonym). Poets often become known by one of these names only.

ARIMA AKITO b. 1930. An outstanding scientist and former president of Tokyo University, Arima Akito was Minister of Education, Science, Sports and Culture from 1998–2000. He was chairman of the Haiku International Association (of Japan). For more, see *Einstein's Century*, ed. L. Gurga and E. Miyashita, Brooks Books, Decatur, 2001.

MATSUO BASHŌ 1644–94. Bashō's pseudonym means 'banana tree' because one grew near his hut. His family was the lowest rank of samurai, little more than farmers. As a *renga* master he travelled widely, sometimes dressed as a monk. For his travel journals and essays (*haibun*), see *The Narrow Road to the Deep North and other travel sketches*, ed./trans. N. Yuasa, Penguin, 1966. For his *renga*, see *The Monkey's Raincoat*, trans. W. Wyatt, Hub, 1998.

YOSA BUSON 1716–83. Equally talented as both poet and painter, Buson dissipated his family estates in pursuit of a literary and artistic career. He took inspiration from Bashō, whose works he illustrated. His haiku are distinguished by a sensuous painterly quality. For more, see *The Path of Flowering Thorn*, by M. Ueda, Stanford UP, 1998.

CHIGETSU d. 1708. The most talented female poet in the Bashō school.

CHIYO-NI 1703–75. Or Chiyo-jo, is regarded as Japan's most celebrated female haiku poet. At the age of fifty-two she became a nun; taking vows allowed her to associate in a socially acceptable way with the male poets. Nonetheless her haiku reflect Buddhist tenets. For more, see *Chiyo-ni – Woman Haiku Master*, by P. Donegan and Y. Ishibashi, Tuttle, 1998.

HINO SŌJŌ 1901–56. Sōjō studied law and then worked in insurance which restricted his opportunities for creative writing. After suffering wartime hardships, he became an invalid.

ICHIKU 1710(?)–60.

INAHATA TEIKO b. 1931. The granddaughter of Takahama Kyoshi, Teiko is still influential as the chair of the Traditional Haiku Society in Japan which she established in 1987. She converted mid-life to Catholicism.

KOBAYASHI ISSA 1762–1826. His pseudonym means 'one cup of tea'. Born on a farm, he was raised by a harsh stepmother and dogged by misfortune and poverty, yet found comfort in the companionship of the smallest living creatures with whom he empathised. For more, see *The Spring of My Life*, trans. S. Hamill, Shambhala Centaur Editions, Boston, 1997, and *The Autumn Wind*, trans. L. Mackenzie, Kodansha, 1984.

KANEKO TŌTA b. 1919. After university and employment in a bank, Tōta's career was interrupted by naval service in the Pacific during World War II. He is a leading exponent of avant-garde haiku with human interest and has produced a liberal *saijiki* including season words from the urban-human environment. He is a former President of Modern Haiku Association in Japan.

TAKARAI KIKAKU 1661–1707. A protégé of Bashō, who criticised his desire to astonish the reader with unusual observations.

KITŌ 1741–89. A disciple of Buson with a straightforward style. He was fond of drink and became a monk.

KYORAI 1651–1704. An associate of Bashō, Kyorai was the son of a Confucianist and fond of martial arts.

KYORIKU 1656–1715. A *samurai* and disciple of Bashō, whom he taught to paint. Controversially, Kyoriku separated topics suited to classical poetry from those suited to haiku. His contemporary, Kyorai, countered with this: 'anything can be a haiku topic; any place can be a poetic place in haiku; there is no word that haiku cannot use'. Kyorai's view prevails.

TAKAHAMA KYOSHI 1874–1959. Denying himself a college education, Kyoshi set up a firm to publish haiku books and became Japan's most influential haiku poet in the first quarter of the 20th century. He was very prolific, also writing novels, short stories and essays. He set the natural landscape as the main domain of haiku. He was also the founder of the haiku magazine, *Hototogisu*.

NOMURA TOSHIRŌ b. 1911. A high school teacher and leader of a haiku group.

OGINO YŌKO. After graduating in 1958, Yōko became a Japanese language teacher for the US State Department. She is one of a few Japanese who sometimes write haiku in English for preference, as here.

UEJIMA ONITSURA 1661–1738. Onitsura worked to elevate haiku to a more serious form of poetic expression, employing the concept of 'sincerity', and was admired by Buson.

RYŌKAN 1758–1831. A Zen priest and expert calligrapher, Ryōkan is best regarded for his *tanka*.

AKUTAGAWA RYŪNOSUKE 1892–1927. A teacher of English who also wrote short stories and translated W.B. Yeats into Japanese. The haiku on p. 76 was written for his doctor on the eve of his suicide.

TANEDA SANTŌKA 1882–1940. Santōka's pseudonym means 'burning mountain peak'. After a traumatic early life, including his own failed suicide, he became an exponent of free-style haiku, whilst living the life of a mendicant, itinerant (and often inebriated) Zen monk. For more, see *Mountain Tasting*, trans. J. Stevens, Weatherhill, New York, 1980.

SHADŌ d. 1737. A doctor and disciple of Bashō.

MASAOKA SHIKI 1867–1902. Shiki is a pen-name meaning 'cuckoo'. Born into a low-ranking samurai family, he was impoverished by his father's early death. He left university without a degree and became a newspaper reporter, then a war correspondent. However, tuberculosis rendered him a semi-invalid for most of his short life, so he devoted himself to literature. For more, see *Masaoka Shiki* by J. Beichman, Kodansha, 1986.

KUROYANAGI SHŌHA 1727–71. A hermit who associated with Buson.

SUZUKI MASAJO b. 1906. Masajo has led an eccentric lifestyle, renouncing her marriage to live with her lover, thus impoverishing herself financially and socially. Her haiku are unusual too, in that she has taken the theme of love, traditionally more at home in the thirty-one-syllable *tanka* form, and made it the subject of haiku. For more, see *Love Haiku*, trans. L. Gurga and E. Miyashita, Brooks Books, Decatur, 2000.

TEISHITSU 1610–73. A paper merchant and musician of Kyōto.

MATSUNAGA TEITOKU 1571–1653. A classical scholar, Teitoku wrote allusively, and saw haiku as a way for both commoner and *samurai* to better understand the literary classics.

FURTHER READING

Blyth, R.H. (1949): *Haiku* (4 vols), Hokuseido Press, Japan.

Blyth, R.H. (1963): *A History of Haiku*, Hokuseido Press, Japan.

Shirane, H. (1998): *Traces of Dreams – Landscape, Cultural Memory and the Poetry of Bashō*, Stanford University Press, USA.

Ueda, M. (1992): *Bashō and His Interpreters*, Stanford University Press, USA.

Higginson, W.J. and Harter, P. (1985): *The Haiku Handbook*, Kodansha, Japan.

Modern Haiku Association (of Japan), ed. (2001): *Japanese Haiku 2001*, Gendai Haiku Kyōkai, Tokyo, Japan.

Cobb, D. and Lucas, M. (eds.) (1998): *The Iron Book of British Haiku*, Iron Press, UK.

Swede, G. and Brooks, R. (eds.) (2000): *Global Haiku: Twenty-five Poets Worldwide*, Iron Press, UK and Mosaic Press, Canada.

RESOURCES

The British Haiku Society, Sinodun, Shalford, Braintree, Essex CM7 5HN. Publishes a quarterly journal, *Blithe Spirit*, and a *Haiku Kit* for school teachers.
Website: www.BritishHaikuSociety.org.uk

The Poetry Library, Level 5, Royal Festival Hall, London SE1.
Website: www.poetrylibrary.org.uk

Museum of Haiku Literature, 3-28-10 Hyakunin-cho, Shinjuku-ku, Tokyo 160, Japan.

The Haiku Society of America, P.O. BOX 1260, Hot Springs, AR 71902-1260, USA.
Website: www.hsa-haiku.org

Haiku Canada, #102-40 Dixington Crescent, Toronto (Ontario), M9P 2K8, Canada.